Backstroking
All Night
in the
Starpool

by

Nancy Rose

Published by
Chestnut Hill Publishing, LLC
P.O. Box 322
Stanford, Kentucky 40484

This book may be purchased at your local bookstore or by credit card at
www.chestnuthillpublishingllc.com

First edition printing, January, 2016

Nancy A. Rose
Backstroking All Night in the Starpool
ISBN Number: 978-0-9970341-0-3
Library of Congress Number: 2015957104

Cover design by Paul B. Osborne

For my mother

Maxine Stevens Rose

In memory

It may be that when we no longer know
which way to go
that we have come to our real journey.

The mind that is not baffled is not
employed.

The impeded stream is the one that
sings.

Wendell Berry

Foreword

Why do you write?

I come from a long line of storytellers that includes my mom, her brothers and sisters, and my brothers Bucky, John and Tom. I remember rolling on the floor gasping, begging Bucky to stop talking long enough to catch my breath. My sister Liz and I tell our stories through writing. When a poem wakes me up at four in the morning, I get up and write it down. It's a good feeling when a poem feels right.

How did you come to poetry?

This question stopped me cold … but the "fire" of poetry set me reflecting. When I was ten, writing was a way of being with the quiet despondency in our home in a coalmining town. I sat at my mom's sewing machine, looking out the winter window, and wrote about birds, not about what I was feeling. I loved reading and language, and found magic and escape in the 398 section of the library. In high school I loved memorizing poems. By the time I was in college, I read poetry every night. Some years later, I learned from David Long to experiment with poetic form. Reaching for a line beat or internal or external rhyme took me to language and thought I might never have considered. When a few of us created an outdoorsman's club for high school students, Gary

Burt said whatever we ask of our students, we would first do ourselves. I took this philosophy into my teaching. Every poetry task I set for my students, I set for myself.

Are the poems true?

Yes, as true as I know. My intent is to have a poem recreate a moment, to take me back to the feeling as I experienced it. There is a kind of magic in that process. When the poem works, there is an aesthetic "high" as it moves toward feeling finished, complete. There is satisfaction in having a poem do what I intend. There is also satisfaction when a poem works for others.

CONTENTS

Part I

Someone I loved once gave me
a box full of darkness.

It took me years to understand
that this, too, was a gift.

Mary Oliver, *Thirst*

Soft Air

—for Judy and Justin

The soft air of a Kentucky spring
Breathes deep
Refreshes memory

Lit by early morning sun
Bluebirds and cardinals
Dart and sing in wayside brambles
Finches bounce on forsythia

Greening hills
Highlighted by pink redbud
Glistening on dark branches

Further up
Strata upon strata of
Snow-white dogwood
Heaven

Beautiful Hands

These are hands that connect me to my mother
To the grandmother who loved me
To the great-grandmother I want to know
Once tapered fingers wear heavy knuckles
And after a hard day the veins
Stand up and shout, *Let go!*
I listen and remember
In freezing cold my mother hung
Fresh washed and steaming Levis on the line
After dark, I brought them in
Stood them behind the stove to thaw
Today my mother's hands curl in resistance
They won't obey her
They say, *No!* to *should* and *have to*
They say, *No more!*
To heavy aching loss
As the echo in my mother's hands
Begins to sound in mine
I long to fill them up
With bouquets of lavender and roses
With music
With connection that warms
And soothes and releases
Let these hands embrace soft things
Let them create
Let them comfort and console
Let them dance
Let them lift up my heart
Let them lift up a mirror so bright
That the love of all the grandmothers
Shines through
Let them heal

Kindness Undoes Me

After saying a 'No, but thank you' when he asked
Are there any other questions I can answer for you?
I hung up quickly as racking sobs shook my body

I have heard those sounds before
They are deep grief coming out
They still startle me, but they no longer scare me

They will subside and I will feel the physical release
Of visceral weight
And wonder why

What are the unspoken questions
That a stranger's kindness answers
In a way the heart can accept

Appalachia

Appalachia is hard on the heart
Sad dogs tied on short rope
Fighting chicken shelters in a row

Yard art a huge boulder
Cuddling the hood of a car
Twenty years now

A tornado's path
Trees swept down one hillside
And up another

Mountains moved by machines
Stripped of coal
Some used locally
Most shipped out

Like other resources
Including people

Voices of Memory

Who am I
When I come home with no plan in my head
When the line between activity and stupor
Is so thin
Where are the infinite possibilities
The thousand and one things

The line wavers
The phone rings
I wake up two hours later
Curled under a comforter
Cat behind my knees
What are the rituals of my days
Where are the ancestral ways
I hunger for

Sanctuary

I accompanied my uncle at milking time
In the evening light his voice was soft
As were the sounds of the animals
Who welcomed us
Their primal music and the fragrance of their bodies
Made the barn a sanctuary, a holy place
First he would fill my smaller pail
With communion for the cats
Then he would take aim at me
Anointing my open mouth
Until I'd sputter and giggle with delight
After returning to the house
We'd strain the milk and pour it warm
Over bowls of cornbread broken into little pieces
Then sit on the back steps with a spoon
And watch the stars come out

Memorial Days

Pleasant Hill, air sweet with honeysuckle
Yielded wild roses and Queen Anne's Lace
Dust patterns on patent leather buckles
Dust streaks on the sweaty, sunburned face
Of cousin after cousin whose arms were laden
With field flowers for Grandma and Uncle Cecil
Who died in World War I and went to heaven
And Uncle Tom, who was murdered with a sickle

Today at Conrad Gardens flags announce
Turn left beyond the vets past cradle row
We kneel on lawn and pull the holder out
And fill the vase with flowers and then we go
The dust on my Adidas I brought with me
There's one bird dropping on George Summertree

Ten Days Later
… for Tom

Kentucky is crying this morning
Gentle tympani in a driveway puddle
Loud drops from a tall oak pound on the roof
Resound on the weight in my heart
Birds flit from dogwood berries to holly trees
And grey squirrels continue their October gathering

This is your land
You are now, even more, a part of its spirit
Small peace in a quiet, gentle lull
Then the wind blows in a new gust of grief
And spirit bubbles dance in the driveway
My guess is, you are smiling

Mom

Last night I was thinking
Either you are going to die before I do
Or I'm going to die before you do
Either way, the illusion of separation
Seems unbearable
How could I possibly live through that experience
I cannot imagine life without my mother
Dying before you feels like it would be easier
Except for how sad that would make you
Has made you
Because I can hardly get my heart and
Mind around it
I don't dwell much on how painfully
Devastating it must be to lose a child
And I don't want to know what it's like
To lose a mom

So, don't go!
Stay here forever and ever!
Working with kids keeps you young
So take my job!
I'll travel and socialize with the senior citizens
And sing them to dinner
If you'll teach me your songs
What this poem boils down to
Is a way to say I love you
            I love you   I love you
If I shouted it from a mountain top
Every minute for the rest of my life
It would not be enough
            I love you   I love you
If I go before you
I'll shout it from the other side
            I love you   I love you

That is, when I'm not trying to catch my breath
From laughing at Bucky's stories
Or running with my dogs or
Telling my cat she's beautiful
Or hugging Grandma or hanging out
With Aunt Jewell and Tick
Maybe we'll all be yelling, *I love you!*
In one big chorus
And, I know, if you go before me
You'll take time out from all that
Socializing, laughing, dancing, and telling stories
To touch me softly
So that my head and heart will know
You are near

No Blinding Light

Some days I find it hard to write a poem
No soul within, within
So I put pen away and wait another day 'til
Thoughts of home
Bring space and time to comb the tribal memory
So to ken
The relationship of self to end
I hone that line and call it poem

That's not the way I'd like to write
It's a hard adventure
Sitting up at night
I'd rather the blinding light
Of inspiration supplied the clincher
I'd scan that list of words and call it right

Acceptance Notice

I want to kiss
Someone
Put my arms
Around
Another human
And say
I love you

I'd like to
Hug someone
Lean into friendly form
Tuck my chin
On warm shoulder
And say
Nothing at all

Turpentine
— for Uncle Roy

Listen to that high voice
That's ole Suze and there goes ole Cannonball
Hear him lowin'
I'm seventeen and then twenty-seven
My brothers and I have followed our favorite uncle
Up a dark mountain trail by carbide mining light
We build a small fire for warmth
Not big enough to obscure our view of the
Night sky
The dogs run
Baying their let's-get-going song
Later they pick up the fox's scent and
The chorus goes wild
Our uncle listens and
Like a Navajo code talker tells us

That's ole Cannonball
Comin' along the ridge and gettin' close
There's ole Suze comin through the cane brake
Headin' for the piney woods
What's ole Jake doin' down in the holler?
Git up there, boy!

We'll lie out listening until
We're too cold or too sleepy
Then head for home
Knowing the dogs will be in by morning
We'll go looking for any stragglers after breakfast
Doctor their paws with turpentine if they're limping

Pulling our blankets closer
We listen to long ago stories
While soaking up the spaces between the stars

As a late moon comes up our uncle says
You know that story about a man on the moon
That's just made up, you know
There's no man up there walking around

The voices of that night and
The hounds are distant now
But their music still plays in my head
In the spaces between the stars
Real as moonlight and wind
I hear their symphony

Christmas Clock

I received the gloves the Christmas I was ten
From that time on I knew there was an end
To any chance of being a carefree child
Of roaming hills with my brothers running wild
My mother handed them to me on Christmas Eve
As the two of us set out Santa's gifts around the tree
Red velvet mittens edged in soft white fur
A grown up present for a not yet grown up girl
On Christmas morning
Which would be coming soon
Three boys and a baby girl would
Rush from their rooms
I would be excited for the younger children to see
What lay for them beneath the festive tree
This triggering thought brought memories of
Christmases past
Of earlier years when I too woke before dawn
To spy the hidden treasure and look upon
The magic our parents had woven for each of us
My mind edged toward the future sensing fear
How would life be for us in coming years
Where was the absent father I longed to see
Why was I taking his place at this year's tree
Mom said when the magic for the kids
Was finally complete
That Christmas for her would be
Just to get off her feet
Even at ten I knew her role was heavy
Who tended the child's heart of this noble lady
It was after midnight when we made our way to bed
No sugar plums or dreams danced in my head
I felt as though the song somehow had stopped
As if a hand had stilled the Christmas clock

Purple Heart

Cut the trees, Henry
Aunt Alkie said when she
Could no longer climb the hill

As soon as the stone was set
She wanted to see it
Through the long dark winters

On top of her piano
Sat the photo of the soldier
Decorated and distant

The cross that she sang about
Was not only far away on a hill
But also in her heart

A mother's heart has to be big enough
To carry her grief
To dust the pictures on the piano

To look up at the stone on the hill
Then turn to greet her grandson
Who carries the same name

No Life Line

He was my father
And after a year of being sober
He had wrecked his car Memorial weekend
And he was leaving

He came out of the house with his suitcases
Tossed them in the car
And turned to say goodbye

We stood huddled in the yard
My mother and five children
Tears streaming down our faces
Our bodies shaking
Daddy, don't go . . . Don't go, Daddy
Don't go . . . Don't go

With the sound of the car's engine
The space capsule that was our family exploded
The individual astronauts doubled over
In their unbearable pain
Silently drifting away from each other

Choice

Like bands around a barrel
Feelings locked in muscles constrict the body
Full breath won't come
Like wine, the body needs to breathe

Fear ferments
Rises to the top in relationship
With self
With others

Holding on to the illusion of control
Decants bitter dregs of regret

Releasing fear
Breathing deeply
The fullness of self

Running

In an after school whirl of movement
I step down from the bus
Change my clothes
Leap from the porch and cross the road
Running full bore into the hills
Up and breathing hard
Gaining momentum as I climb
The heat of sandstone rising
The heat of the sun coming down
Up and breathing deep
Swiftly over logs cushioned in tall grass
Up and over boulders
My feet sticking sure
Late afternoon air currents lift my hair
Cool my neck
Legs stretch as I skirt the cemetery fence
And move under a canopy of trees
Pine needles and mosses fill my senses
And then it comes
The breath that fills all my being
Every part of my mind
That cleanses and then releases
The second wind that trumpets to all of my synapses
This body can run forever
In perfect harmony with itself and the earth
And whatever life brings
No more constrained classrooms
No more reaching for words
That won't matter tomorrow
No more lines on my mother's face
From no letter from my father
Along a leaf littered trail
In dappled light
I run

Travelers

I sit in a willow tree
And I am ten
Following the sounds of the
Occasional passing car
Some world traveler
I'd think
Heading for Ipanema or
Some other place Snookie Lansing
Sings about on The Hit Parade

Tonight I sit on my porch
Wishing for more space
Between passing cars
Travelers, I think, who most likely
Want to find home

Med

When Med picked up Nancy Elizabeth
So they could start their life together
He owned his horse, his saddle, and
Clothes in his saddlebags

Hard work and children later
He ordered material to build a new home
According to his youngest
People passing on the road
Stopped to watch

Why, I asked
Because he built it with so many large windows
Why did he do that
I guess he just liked light

Mother Mine

Your healing heart
Is a Valentine
One hundred percent love
Courage and grace
You warm our hearts
With your smiling face
Your funny stories make us laugh
You take us on trips into the past
No sky miles from Delta
Just tales about relatives
We would never know them
These parts of ourselves
If you didn't tell us
We'd miss all this wealth
You are our window
To souls who've taken flight
Just like your father
You *let in the light*

Apple Leaves Promise

All winter
Two leaves have lingered
In the top of the apple tree

Through storms of ice, snow,
Rain, sleet, hail and wind
They remain

Do they like the winter view
Is it their two-ness that
Keeps them together

What heartbeat marks
The time of their departure

Did they make a vow
That neither would remain alone

What inner voice
Keeps the heart
Long after the body's prime
Is gone

Part II

I caught the happy virus last night
When I was out singing beneath the
stars.

It is remarkably contagious —
So kiss me.

Hafiz, *The Subject Tonight is Love*

Sterling

After running through a hard rain
I was sitting on the floor of Joan's studio
When Sterling came in to pick up his violin
Play something for me, I said
I'll play if you will, he said
But I don't play, I laughed
He smiled, play the piano
But I don't play the piano
Then play my violin and I'll play the piano
And he held it out to me
Panicked, I ran across the white carpet on my knees
And sat down at the grand piano
What, I asked
Just start, he said
Joan, Help! Aren't you going to get your Cello?
Nope, she said sitting down
Holding on to her hands and knees to contain herself
I'm going to listen
I looked at Sterling, he nodded
I began
And he came in
The music carried us
Into another world
So immediate, so beautiful
After a bit, Joan could not resist
She ran from the room and returned
Cello and bow in hand
We were a trio
First one leading, then another
We were within the music
In the middle of a universe
Where sunlight washes a bright evening
After a hard rain

Blues

I was so tired last night
I just wanted to go home
I tell you, I was tired last night
I could hardly move my bones

Drove home in a summer rain
Let my cat out of the door
Drove home in that light summer rain
To find piled up dishes and a dirty floor

Oh, yeah
I was tired last night

Night Sentinel

The white cat leaped down from the glider and
Walked purposefully across the deck and
Down the steps
To the edge of the graveled drive
Two large ghost-like deer
Stood silently watching her approach
Beneath the towering legs
Beside their tiny hooves
She paused and looked up
The antlered heads in unison
Bowed to her nose
In ancient starlit greeting
Her task complete she retraced her steps
And the night visitors entered my rose garden

Didgeridoo

I want to be a didgeridoo player
A circular breather who takes in oxygen
Until I'm a hundred and two
I want my body to vibrate to those low tones
Until it lets go of all dis-harmony
Until my mind floats as free
As all that throbbing sound
Getting down
Getting down
Drone on ole Didgeri
I've got the blues
And you are good news

Full Spring Tumble

Raindrops pool on the roof of my tent
Run down the sides like shooting stars
Like comets
Like tadpoles skittering to secret hideaways

Here in a sweet corner of the world
Thirty-five young poets follow their muse

Collectively and individually
They skitter to special spots
To tent sites
To a rocky lakeshore
A forest trail, a waterfall
To campfires and drum circles
Pushed by secret and not-so-secret longings
To connect with each other
With themselves
With the beauty of this place
Written and unwritten
The poems begin

The steady pelting rain competes
With the endless roar of the falls
With laughter and voices
And, thank heaven, mostly wins
Over the music in Ryan's truck

The thoughts in my head
Compete with my intent to write
With an insistent urge to sleep
What cacophony, what symphony
My heart is singing
And sleep, I think, is winning

The raindrops on the lake
Are so light I don't
Feel them on my skin
Being here feels complete
I don't want to write or think
Or tend to any lingering detail

I want to sit back, let go
And soak up the beauty
Of friends huddled together for warmth
Of swimmers dipping in a snowmelt lake
Of bonfire builders, coffee brewers
Of guitar strummers and hand drummers
Of dreamers and singers

I want to soak up the evening song of birds
The roar of the falls
The gangliness of a brown baby moose
The warm affection of playful pup
Bad Bad Leroy Brown

As memory folds upon memory
I want to embrace
And be embraced by these people
To hang on to this experience

Someone throws fresh logs on the fire
It's after midnight
And the continuous drizzle
Has not dampened the spirits
Of poets who read, recite
Dance, sing, then read and dance some more

Something has begun here
A weaving of a web so intricate
That it empowers its weavers
To spin with thread from their hearts
To spin improvisationally
To pull their pasts into the present
To co-create a pattern that says:
This is who we are
We are becoming ourselves
This celebration is within us

Sparks fly up
Firelight illuminates these faces
This night

Ah, Jared

You find the perfect raspberry
Show me its beautiful symmetry
Then break it in half
Sweet communion

Early Morning

Morning, Mister Sun
You are up before me
You did not dance last night
  …

I see my shadow
Passing golden willow trees
I must be alive
  …

Ho, Baby Otter
I miss your quick morning smile
You are my touchstone
  …

Morning pond reflects
Bouquets of golden willows
Thank you, Grandfather
  …

Red-winged blackbird sings
Fluffy bowing cattail song
To secret nestlings
  …

New green cattail shoots
Springing eternal like hope
Cycle of life, poem

El Gato

Soft and silver
Your highlights play
Like magic halos
Around your blue grey body
You are nine pounds small
And regal in your dense fur
A Modigliani poised
On a baby grand piano
Ancient Egyptians
Called you Bastet
Goddess of happiness
Your gaze holds my eyes
Soul deep and unwavering
Do you dream of Granada
When you lie sleeping in the sun
The sounds of Flamenco in the night
Your relatives minding the streets
Below the Alhambra
Are you content
To tend a solitary house all day
To lead me to your dishes
When they need to be filled
To the door for your brief exits
Into winter
I like the songs you sing
When you curl into me at night
After the winter moon is up
And there's enough starlight in the yard
For you to go off duty

In the Night

Night is the color of mystery
Of the way my soul sinks down
And waits
Of clouds that drift
And feelings that surface
If I listen
I can hear voices
They bring comfort
Give me space
Say what needs
To be said
If I sit long enough
I will feel night's blessing
The trees will talk to me
And my soul will know
When it's time to go

I'll Be There at Six

You can be the hors d'oeuvres, he says
As I respond to his invitation
To see his slides on Tibet

You're a friend, I say laughing
Yes, he says, we've slept in the same tent
And hiked beautiful trails, I say
And I want to do it again

Me, too, he says
I've got to strengthen my back
Me too, I say
My whole body

I'll be there at six, I say
And hang up smiling

Dark Horses

Dark horses
Running across
The plains of my dreams

Dark horses
Under a night sky
Full of stars

Poised on their backs
I dance
In sync with moving muscle
Music from their hooves
Echoes from distant canyon walls

Breathing out
Breathing in
I bathe
In the fragrance of the night

Balanced
Beyond waking

Shri Ram Jay Ram
— for Kent

May the monkey king
Use the strength of all who love you
To rip up the right mountain
And lay at your feet
The flower that heals you
And may you take it up
With the grace
That is so much a part
Of your magnificent being

Donta's Poem

Icicles? Icicles!
Lullabies? Lullabies!

Two new words for a two-year-old to own
Like *Airplane...* and *Blue moon*

Airplane song! Sing the airplane song!

Up, up and away...
In Donta's little airplane
Up, up and away...
He flies in the sky all day

Jet trails fade, the sky darkens
Child, each time I look at you, you are taller
Blue moon? you say and nod your head

In the silence behind the mountains,
The moon rises, trailing faint notes of lullabies

Like Frosty the snowman, the icicles are melting
Leaving puddles in my heart

My Old Failures

When my old failures
Gang up on me
I feel sad
Or intensely alone

If I ignore them long enough
I am overwhelmed
By prickly anger

What I wish for is
A spiral of dance
I can move into
One that wraps me inside
A center of warmth
And music and light
And dances me through fear
Into a place of wild, wild abandon
Then back to the center of myself

Breathe, She Said

In search of a mirror
I can climb into
I dive deep
Then rise to swim languidly on a lake
Water dropping
Like pebbles from my arms.
With each stroke the water pulls back my hair
Clears cobwebs of care I brought with me
Sloughs away vestiges of not-me energy
I don't know how to cut loose
In my daytime world.
Breathe! she says.
But I'm breathing, I say.
And with each breath
I both run from feeling
And memory
And return to myself

November Symphony
                    —for John

Snow geese ...
          formation after formation of them
A shining sky symphony
Of silver notes edged in blue
Filling the sky with their song
In November sun
Below, three of us walk a pipeline road
Along a field of winter grain
Montana and Tennessee in Colorado
Convening with snow geese for Thanksgiving

I ask my brother for his wire cutters
Carried in his back pocket
From early morning feeding
Of sweet smelling hay
To bouncy calves, black cows and powerful bulls
My sister holds on to the back of my jacket
As I lean over an irrigation ditch and cut
Thick stems of tall weeds topped with spiky balls

Back at the house we arrange them
In a black rubber feed tub
Weighted with a spool of barbed wire
We add dried thistles, lavender scented sage
And tall grass spikes
Plumed with fluffy blond heads
Then sit back in the sun
To drink hot chocolate
Scan the sky for more snow geese
And admire our work

Today I'm Living in a Poem

Riding the chairlift at Blacktail with Mari
She says the clouds are racing to New Zealand
To see her father
In this white sanctuary
Incense rises from Doghair pine
And snow ghosts silently bless us
Near the top strong winds gust and heave
Like wild ocean waves
Skis whoosh and slide and souls dance
While the sun pushes blue sky
And tears around my face

The Jewel

Ah, Aeneas
Across February snow
My soul reaches out to you
Breathing hard
I climb your steep, green paths
Spin three hundred and sixty degrees
On top of your view of the world
Drop down in the sun
On your warm mountain heart
And sleep contented sleep
Until awakened
By a baby mountain goat
Snuffling my eyelashes

Rumi and Ecstatic Living

This morning before dawn
I drink lemon tea, eat toasted almond bread
And watch two horses silhouetted
Against the snow
Raring up playfully with each other
Weaving an inverted V of black lace
Against the white background
Even confined in a field
Theirs is not a treadmill life

As Homer's rosy-fingered dawn paints the space
Between Teakettle and Columbia mountains
Deep in Glacier Park, Heaven's Peak emerges
Darkly blue
Below, twinkling lights of civilization
Softly highlight the tableau
And the horses turn toward the rising sun
For breakfast

And Then ...

I have this vision of living in my car
Camping at the foot of enormous mountains
Swimming to bird call
While lathered in evening light
Then falling asleep
Under a splendid night sky

I am forgetting to use language
Or call your name

Night Music

Hey, firelight music
Your playful beat says get up and dance
Move my body so freely
Every creak and groan is gone
Drum vibrations moving through me
Taking me out of my body
Into a wide night sky

I've been wanting all summer
To climb into the Big Dipper
And swim all night in the star pool
Backstroking with the northern lights
Dancing overhead

I would come back
Resplendent in moonlight
Breathing deeply
Trailing stars
Oh, yes

Part III

Where we have stopped dancing, singing, being enchanted by stories, or finding comfort in silence is where we have experienced the loss of soul.

Dancing, singing, storytelling, and silence are the four universal healing salves.

Gabrielle Roth

Rappelling Kila Cliffs with Black Berets

Of course, we'll do everything we ask the kids to do.
    — Gary Burt

Pros, with precision, lay out equipment
The rest of us study the lay of the rock
It's early morning
Too early for conversation
Warm clothes are adjusted
Jokes exchanged
Quiet laughter under trees
Doubled ropes, pulling strong,
Are lined over cliff face to
Two men below
Looking serious and small
My mind is chanting
Practice knots, tie seat harness, snap in carabiner
It's cold, damp, and Saturday
I could be home
Dusting furniture or
Potting geraniums
What?
Yes, I'm ready
Rope through carabiner
Rope around body
Left hand up
Release with right
Stand on cliff's edge
Lean far back
On belay!
Don't look down
Keep leaning . . . . .keep leaning
Body perpendicular
Vibram on granite
An ant's view of heaven!

Kick out . . . . . Release . . . . . Fall

Kick out . . . . . Release . . . . . Fall

It works!   I'm sailing!

Kick out . . . . . Release . . . . . Fall

Hello small cows!

Kick out . . . . . Release . . . . . Fall

Oh, glorious morning!

Kick out . . . . . Release . . . . . Fall

What? I'm down?

Off belay!

Watch your step
The two men are smiling

I've climbed mountains
And slept in snow caves
Rafted rivers and written poems
But nothing compares with rappelling
Down a cold gray cliff
In early morning

About School

He walks backwards on his way to school
A small munchkin in a hooded sweatshirt
Who sits down in the middle of the sidewalk
To think, hands on his cheeks, elbows on his knees

Or … meanders into a yard
Puts his hands and arms
Through a fence and embraces a dog
Three times his size
His smile and the vigorous tail-wagging
Speaking volumes about connection

On another morning he shakes hands
With a trailing, weeping willow branch
Then raises his face and closes his eyes
To receive tumbling … dancing … yellow leaves

Or, arms outstretched and eyes closed,
He twirls slowly … around …
And around … and around
In the frosty billowing exhaust of a warming car

In the pre-dawn hour on Meridian
I agree with him about school

Living and Dying Secondarily

There are two questions
I've been wanting to ask:
Why is school (sometimes)
Oppressive, dull, and sad
And who (or what) decrees
That it be this way

There is an obvious and felt difference
In an atmosphere that is
Safe, open, nurturing, and
Builds community and
One that causes people
To shut down
And desperately want to escape
What exercises of power
Make the concept of community
A joke

Second question:
What is the antidote
To toxicity that attacks the soul
What class can I sign up for
That leaves me whole

I Think I Am Tired…

I think I am tired of being an English teacher
I don't want to be a puppet on a string
I teach the necessity of using one's own mind
How can I not use my own

I want to hang glide in a lazy afternoon
Let my mind and being drift and float
Until I am clear and whole
Ready to dance and speak from my heart

I want to give love and support
To those who are unfurling their wings
To make the sky safe for their venturing
For deciding to dream
For solo flight

Tonka in G 106

My oak desk rose up
Gathered my students' papers
Danced across the floor
Tossed them all out the window
Sat down, crossed his legs and laughed

"Success is counted sweetest ..."

       I feel successful ...
When my cat lets me clip her nails peacefully
When I have dug the tree roots out of my flowerbed
When my kitchen table holds nothing
But a small vase of flowers
When I walk barefoot on clean floors
When the grass is green
When I receive a letter from an old friend
When I am still and bathed in sunrise
When my school room is clean and orderly
When I watch clouds drift
       as evening fades to night
When I stay awake to see a shooting star
And fall asleep in the Big Dipper

Kara's Poem

In Kara's book
I wrote
May the new year
Bring you insights
And fond memories

Then later thought
Insight is born
Of pain and sadness

It's right and necessary
To take the next step
Standing still can
Drown you in regret

And the memories –
Can you love the pain
That carves the soul
Hand-rubs regret
To a polished sheen

You'll be changed
You know

Oh, Kara –
Take a deep breath

Dean

There are secrets to be known at dawn
        — after Rumi

A full moon illuminates the snowy Missions
And wisps of white fog sweep the highway
It is quiet as I drive north at 6:00 a.m.
Yesterday was my dear friend Dean's
Memorial service
Today, Sunday, will be the interment
I learn from Holly that when Dean died
The Episcopal woman minister came to the house
To recite a prayer for releasing the spirit
Such a thoughtful send-off
This dignified woman is having
No tributes she said, *Just tell some stories about*
Adventures along life's path
So songs, prayers and readings sing her to heaven
And afterwards, the gatherings and the stories

The sun shines brilliantly drying the grass
Where the snow has been pushed aside
On a green cloth
An elegant black marble box
Beside it a bouquet of flowers
Close by, other bouquets, family and
Friends keep vigil
Two women priests read the comforting psalms
Pour brown earth in the sign of the cross
Over black marble
Then recite the commitment
This is a moment of hard letting go
On all sides, mountains lift up their snowy peaks
To blue heaven ... Alleluia!

Driving home and still today
Tears emerge unexpectedly
With them an awareness begins to make itself clear
What we do to honor Dean is to honor
What was important to her
Her family, her friends, the rewards of travel
A meaningful conversation, and, of course
A well choreographed, or impromptu, good time

Gato

I rock my Gato in my heart
As she lays her heart against mine
Softly puts her paws around my neck
And tucks her head beside my chin
Gato, I say, missing her
Gato, I say, I love you
She nudges my chin
For a kiss on top of her head
Looks at me with clear, knowing eyes
And snuggles closer

Knapweed and Roses

If I could take all the knapweed
Of my old failures and compost it
Through this hard winter of grief
I'd use it in the spring to nurture
Miniature roses for a baby girl
A copper rose for a life-long friend
And blue bachelor buttons for the eyes
Of a seventeen year old boy
If I could have them back again
Knapweed would become
More beautiful than roses

Late Summer in Sandpoint

Looking down on the Pend Oreille
We spot the tiny airstrip
We circle, tie down, and walk over to a seaplane
Listening as its owner talks about maneuvers
For keeping the cockpit free of water

Another pilot offers us a ride into town
With four of us in the front seat of his pickup
He grins and says
I'd like to hold you on my lap to make more room
But I guess I couldn't drive that way
The lodge features Sunday morning brunch
Customers scattered inside and out
We choose a deck table
Part sun, part shade
And look at green grass sloping to white sand
And blue water

White gulls invite the eye and the mind
What land … what time is this
What prehistoric shore or blue Aegean Sea
What is it our spirits are reaching for

Over the bar is a painting in two parts
Is it ocean — is it sky —
What is the activity — the color —
The feeling is of freedom and it calls us back

On the beach a man does Tai Chi
Yang style — long form
Framed by two trees, sun, and water
He could be any time — any place

It's leaving time
We walk through town
Look at dragon kites and Birkenstocks
Taxi back to the airport and head home
Sunday morning in Sandpoint
Is a short distance
To the heart

Mythic Dimensions of Place

The chest of drawers in my bedroom
Is missing its second drawer
Full of cups from the kitchen of my old house
It is downstairs waiting to be unpacked

In this new space I am finding how very little I need
I like the bare white walls
The expanse of hard wood flooring
The cat racing and skidding, chasing her tiny mouse

Yesterday I thought, maybe I just won't unpack
Or at least I'll approach the task very slowly
I want no dead wood on my shelves or
Hanging in my closets
Nothing to haunt me
Nothing to steal my life away
Nothing to wolf down time I could spend dancing
Or walking in the snow

Then at four o'clock this morning
An inanimate device broke loose and flooded
Half the basement
Half the unpacked boxes

Poseidon must be angry
Odysseus, throw me the veil!

End of Summer

My body is moaning from too much activity
Oh how this puppy soul wants to shake out
And read a book
Or drool over hot fudge and huckleberries
That would be a soaring good time
Hey, are you listening

Next Road

Road, I am afraid of you
I don't know where you're going
Where are you leading me
Will I know when I'm there
What am I missing by my holding back
Why can't I see through your haziness
To what am I saying no
Do you make any promises, Road
Can you read my mind
Are there signposts I will understand
That say Calcutta or Katmandu
Is there a destination for this journey
Is it internal
Or external, and possibly wrong
Can you answer one more question
Have I been getting there all along

Ichi Kokoro

This diminutive Japanese woman
How delighted she is
With tall American me
She leads the way through the park
And speaks as if I am intelligent
And can understand her every word
Her smile says she knows
The distance between us
And does not mind
I am a strange and new friend
To whom she gives her small box of caramels
Purchased for the cruise down river
I kneel beside her on one knee for a photograph
And turn to look into dark eyes framed by grey curls
And a brown cloche hat
With both hands
She adjusts my scarf
So it will not blow away in the wind

Birks

I am married to these chocolate brown Birks
With their shiny copper buckles
And crumbling heels
Don't have them rebuilt now
The shoe shop lady said
They'll be more comfortable as they are
Bring them in when you return
So, I wore them to Spain and walked
In hot summer sun
Over patterned cobblestone streets
Into Moorish palaces with intricately vaulted arches
And exquisitely tiled ceilings
Into mosques so large that later conquerors
Built cathedrals inside them
Into orange gardens
Fragrant with late blossoms and overripe fruit
Into sweaty Flamenco classes in whitewashed caves
Where my *zapatos* wore blisters on my feet

At noon in a shady plaza
I kicked off my Birks
And ate gazpacho with friends
After siesta, more intensive classes *en Espanol*
Then *café con leche* on a vine-covered terrace
Flamenco performances don't start until midnight
So we walk narrow alleys to find an Arab tea room
Step out of our shoes, sit on pillows on the floor
And drink sweet tea in tiny cups

On a different night
We climb the steep back way to the Alhambra
Absorbing the magnificent palaces and
Fountains in the moonlight
Then at midnight picnic on ancient walls
After food and much laughter
I stretch out on cool stone and look at the stars
I want to soak in the night music
Right down to the soles of my feet

Later, we walk down through the dark
Then up to the Gypsy Quarter
Home in the wee hours
I kick off my shoes and
Feel the cool white tile with my toes

More faithful than a mythical lover, shoes
You are a part of me

Summer Wine

On a terrace in Spain
We listen to Curro
Poet and mentor to bullfighters

As the moon lights
The palaces of the Alhambra
He begins to recite
Empieza el llanto
De la guitarra.
Begins the crying of the guitar
La Guitarra, I say, Lorca's poem

Down in the darkness
Guitars and deep song ring out
We listen
And drink *tinto de verano*
Summer wine

Blackfeet Running

The runners are coming! The runners are coming!
Blackfeet women who had been stretching
On my blanket jumped up
I bundled gear into the trunk of my car
You're a runner, and you're a runner
Get in the truck!
The man in charge looked at me and said
You're a runner!
And I choked on the last bite
Of my huckleberry muffin
Look at her everybody, she's eating
She's eating, he laughed
Recovering my breath, I caught up with him
I'm not a runner.
You're a runner, he said.
I'm not Blackfeet.
He stopped and looked into my eyes
You're a human being, aren't you?
I nodded and he pointed
I got into the truck

A friend and I had spent a cold night
In our tents at St. Mary's to be here
I had not run for years

When you see the runner coming, start moving
Holding one hand behind you.
Two staffs are coming over the border
The Bloods will keep theirs
That runner will hand over the traveling staff
To the first Blackfeet runner
He will be carrying the staff of the Blackfeet Nation
There will be Eagle feathers
Don't let them touch the ground

At intervals we were dropped off
On the road to Browning
Then the truck was gone
Just the singing insects, the grass, the sky and me
I took a deep breath

Dear Creator
Help me to put one foot in front of the other,
Let me keep breathing and not fall

After a long while I heard a murmuring
A kind of low chant
Behind me the highway went uphill
Steadily the noise grew louder
Through the ripple of heat rising, a wavering image
A lone runner, like an apparition from another time
As I watched, more people appeared on the horizon
Then a large truck with cameras on top

Ready to move yet mesmerized
I focused on the runner
When I could see and hear him breathing
I started running, one hand held back
He came up beside me and reached out
Take them gently, he said
Reverently handing over the long staffs
Then dropping back
I ran …

I could hear myself breathing and feel
Each step hitting the ground
Slowly I became aware that there were runners
Slightly behind and on either side of me
Their eyes focused ahead

I turned my eyes to the Eagle feathers… and realized

> I was not carrying them
> They were carrying me

It is Sadness I Run From

Each night as I knelt by the glowing grates
Of the gas heater in the boys' room
The tears would come as I thought
Of the suffering
People without homes, without food
Little children with no one to love them
My tears were for them, I thought
Not those of us in this small house asleep
Making our peace for another day
Asking hope to counter desperation
Of a disappeared father
Of a hard-working mother
Struggling to put food on the table
To keep the focus on our responsibility
To think of others and be grateful for what we had

The tears were a cleansing
A way to warm one side of my body
Before climbing into the top bunk to sleep
Not so many hours until morning

It is sadness that I run from
It is sadness that brings me home

Alchimista

— For Artemesia Gentileschi (1593-1656)

And when she was ready
She opened her arms like wings
And through her hands
Released the pent-up energy
Of her heart
Fanning the golden flames
She transmuted illusion
And drew to herself
This world
Her lover

Acknowledgements

Many thanks to my family, extended family and friends, who are a source of much joy, and who listen and ask for poems.

Thanks to Donna Marx who asked for my book at bookstores before it was conceived.

Thanks to Emily Ann Smith at Berea College who insisted on "pithy" writing.

Thanks to David Long who put his foot against the door to prevent my leaving when I realized his creative writing class meant writing poetry.

Thanks to Barbara Thomas, Cherokee poet and mentor, who has called my attention to the Native sensibility in my poetry, and asks, "Is your manuscript ready?"

Thanks to my students who continually opened my eyes and heart.

Thanks to Kitty Stoner who created my first poetry book by hand.

Thanks to Justin Turner for saying, "You're a poet!"

Thanks to Joe Zambrano and the audiences at Clementine's and Grill 409.

Thanks to friends who have led, pushed, and cajoled me into new experiences, in music, drama, dance, and travel, on mountain tops and on rivers.

Thanks to Jeanette and Mariya Stangle for Memorial weekend floats and camping at the Homestead.

Thanks to the Creative Women's Circle (Jules, Marsha, Rebecca, Dorothy, Suzie, Maggie, Jamilla, Linda, Jordonna and Leslie) for focus on the creative process and "one sweet thing."

Thanks to my book group of 21 years, COW for Circle of Women, (Julie, Genia, Helen H, Cissy, Helen P, Lynn, Karen, Sarah).

Thanks to Cissy Klein, Mark Shiltz, Ruth Hopkins Zajdel, Carla Hannaford, Genia Allen-Schmid, Kevin Allen-Schmid, Maggie Logan, Gina Rose, Helen Pilling, Sarah Burdick, Liz Rose, Kathy Culbert, Craig Platt, Carol Lindsay, Rima Nickel, Jo Shay, Sharon Berger, Kitty Stoner, Lynn Scalf, Judy Collins, and Judy Turner for perspective on this manuscript.

Thanks to Marsha Sultz, my hiking buddy, for the morning of hiking Mt. Aeneas photo.

Thanks to Skip Via for computer MS technique.

Thanks to the folks at Chestnut Hill for patience, encouragement and guidance.

.

Nancy Rose

Nancy Rose was born on the Carter County, Kentucky farm, and in the bed of her grandmother, Nancy Elizabeth Blevins Stevens, who doctored people. She was named for "Aunt Nance" and her paternal grandmother, Mary Allen "Molly" Womack Rose, a teacher, artist and musician. Reared in eastern Kentucky, she is a graduate of Prestonsburg schools and Berea College, with a B.A. in English. She was secretary in the Political Science Department at the University of Kentucky, before returning to Berea to become Dean of Women in the Foundation School.

Deciding to teach full time, Nancy drove a blue VW bug to Montana and discovered that western Montana is a lot like eastern Kentucky ... beautiful trees, mountains and people. She loved her students, the magic of teaching, seeing the lights go on via poetry, mythology, science fiction, fantasy, modern media and world literature, and she loved spending time out of doors. She spent a summer in an English Institute at the University of Montana, where she began her graduate study, and a summer in the Appalachian Writer's Workshop at Hindman, Kentucky, discovering James Still and his *River of Earth* and Gurney Norman who took her to the local library to check out the only copy of *Divine Right's Trip.*

Nancy has taught in China and traveled in Japan, Spain, the Caribbean, and Italy. She has also taught at Flathead Valley Community College and at the University of Montana. Her poems have appeared in *Mountain Life & Work, The Magazine of the Appalachian South,* and in *Cut-Thru Review,* The Big Sandy Community and Technical College Literary Magazine.